TWELVE ROUNDS TO GLORY

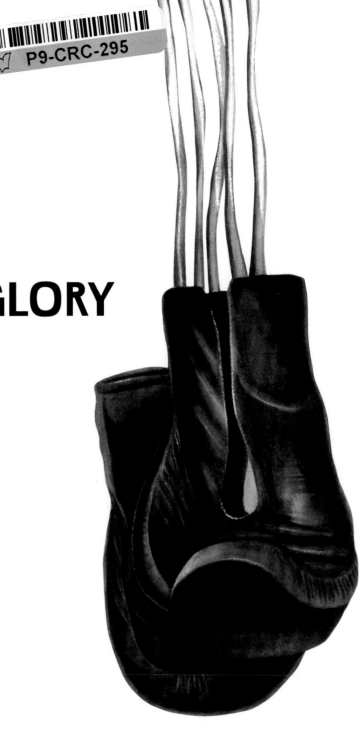

TWELVE ROUNDS
to GLORY
The Story of Muhammad Ali

Charles R. Smith Jr.

illustrated by
Bryan Collier

CANDLEWICK PRESS

This book is dedicated to my dad, my uncles Herbert and Ricky Bain,
and my grandfather Lester Smith, whose memory continues
to inspire me to inspire others.
C. R. S. Jr.

Muhammad Ali is a great champion for the human spirit. He embodies the
wonderful qualities of love, bravery, courage, power, artistry, sacrifice, and service
to humankind. I dedicate this book to the future, and in the last image,
I hope you will note the single black balloon floating to the sky, which represents
Ali's power and fragility. He's still floating, just like in the beginning.
B. C.

Text copyright © 2007 by Charles R. Smith Jr.
Illustrations copyright © 2007 by Bryan Collier

First paperback edition 2010

Library of Congress Cataloging-in-Publication Data

Smith, Charles R., date.
Twelve rounds to glory : the story of Muhammad Ali /
Charles R. Smith Jr. ; illustrated by Bryan Collier — 1st ed.
p.   cm.
ISBN 978-0-7636-1692-2 (hardcover)
1. Ali, Muhammad, 1942– — Juvenile literature.
2. Boxers (Sports) — United States — Biography — Juvenile literature.
I. Collier, Bryan, ill. II. Title.
GV1132.A4S65 2007
796.83092 — dc22   [B]   2007025998

ISBN 978-0-7636-5002-5 (paperback)

16 17 CCP 10 9 8 7 6 5 4

Printed in Shenzhen, Guangdong, China

This book was typeset in Scala.
The illustrations were done in watercolor and collage.

Candlewick Press
99 Dover Street
Somerville, Massachusetts 02144

visit us at www.candlewick.com

Contents

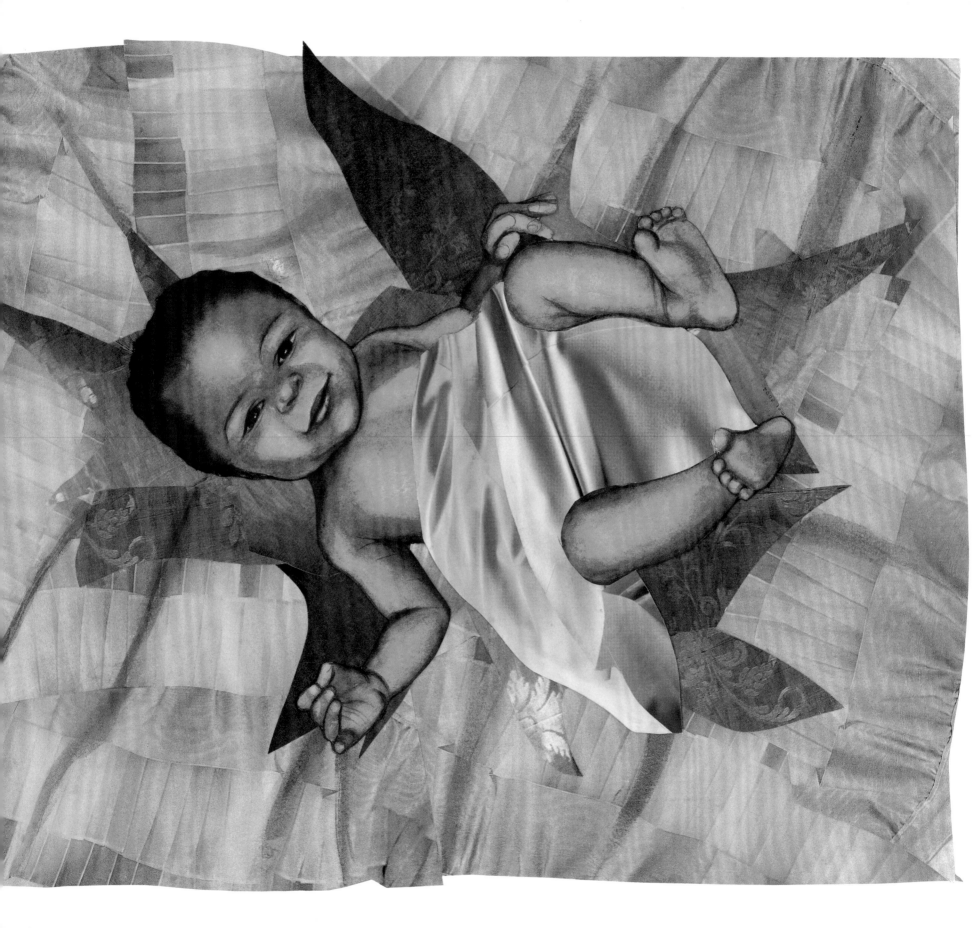

ROUND ONE THE GOLDEN CHILD

**"I always felt like God made Muhammad special,
but I don't know why God chose me to carry this child."**
— ODESSA CLAY, Cassius Clay's mother

Bathed in beautiful light
from parental love,
brown skin shimmers
with a glow from above.
In 1942, the seventeenth of January,
you entered the world
in Louisville, Kentucky.
Whites Only stores
and Whites Only parks
sifted you out
because you were dark.
No Negroes Allowed
and No Colored signs
created separate worlds
and drew color lines,
but your middle-class parents
managed to survive
through hard work and faith
and were able to provide

you, their first child,
and your little brother later,
with food, shelter, clothing,
and something much greater:
love
that was passed
to you from day one,
love
that was passed
to you, the new son
of mother Odessa
and father Cassius Clay,
who also passed the torch
of your name
that birth day,
passed down to you
from a white farmer who
inherited a plantation
and your great-grandfather too.

But Clay freed his forty slaves
during America's dark days,
then fought to end slavery
and fought to change ways
and laws
and thinking
deep in the South,
using newspapers,
knives,
fists,
and his mouth.
He fought with a spirit
that lives in you today,
reflected in your name,
Cassius Marcellus Clay,
reflecting love from your parents,
who had faith and belief
that God would watch over you
and provide inner strength.

ROUND TWO
IGNITING THE FLAME

**"Daddy, I go to the grocery and the grocery man is white.
I go to the drugstore and the drugstore man's white.
The bus driver's white. What do the colored people do?"**
—CASSIUS CLAY, age five

Like father,
like son,
you tried to charm everyone,
a tale-spinning performer
holding court on your porch,
only eight years old,
already carrying the torch
of fire-filled speech,
used to brag,
joke,
and preach
to anyone who would listen,
to anyone within reach.
This skill you would use
later in life,
to taunt your opponents
and draw crowds to your fights.

But first we begin
with the story of a bike,
a brand-new, shiny
Schwinn, red and white,
ridden by you, young Cassius Clay
to a fair one fine day.
But that fine day
turned instantly gray
when you noticed your bike
was stolen away,
a moment that changed
your life in one day;
with tears in your eyes,
you wanted some body to pay.
You found a cop
and went on to say,
"I'm gonna whup whoever it was
that stole my bike!"
The cop replied,
"First, kid, you hafta learn how to fight!"
And fight you did,
at the age of twelve,
taught by that cop,
awaiting your first bell.
After six short weeks
you won by a decision
of two out of three judges,
and to all who would listen,
you declared your goal
to be the "greatest of all time,"

"I'm gonna whup whoever

it was that **stole my bike!"**

"First, **kid,** you hafta **learn** how to **fight!"**

mighty words uttered
from a thin eighty-nine-
pound kid who put
a goal into motion,
by tackling your training
with discipline and devotion.
Mornings began,
rise and shine,
at four
A.M.
for workout time.
A quart of milk
and two raw eggs,
you guzzled for energy
to power your legs.
You trained and ran
and ran and trained,

before school and after
again and again,
believing that boxing
would bring to you
the life of your dreams
because you knew
too many black men
with degrees and education
who couldn't get work
due to racist separation.
Your eyes witnessed men
who drowned their frustration
by drinking and smoking
and partying all night.
You used your frustration
to stoke fire
for fights.

ROUND THREE
CLAY, THE CONQUEROR OF ROME

"To make America the greatest is my goal,
So I beat the Russian, and I beat the Pole,
And for the U.S.A. won the medal of gold.
Italians said, 'You're greater than the Cassius of old.
We like your name, we like your game,
So make Rome your home if you will.'
I said, 'I appreciate your kind hospitality,
But the U.S.A. is my country still,
'Cause they waiting to welcome me in Louisville.'"

—CASSIUS CLAY at the Louisville airport upon returning from Rome

Confident teenager already in control
of mind, body, and spirit,
on the road to your goal,
using mouth, skill, and fire
to fulfill your desire
to become a pro boxer,
you set the limits higher
by pushing opponents
with words before a fight,
launching verbal jabs
and trying to ignite
fear in them
and interest in you,
young Cassius Clay,
the loud boxer who
was quicker than lightning
when bouncing on toes,
using unblinking vision
and fists that flicked foes
thrown from strong shoulders,
landing all over,
recoiling in the ring
and striking like a cobra.
Striking and stinging
with unique boxing form,
you maintained a cool head
in the swirl of fight storms;
you maintained a cool head
that carried you through
amateur ranks

and all the way to
a shot at the Olympics
taking place in Rome,
a plane ride away
from your Louisville home.
A plane ride stood
between you and greatness,
but a deep fear of flying
would be your biggest test.
To the cop who was your coach
you begged and you pleaded,
but after hours of listening
he said that you needed
to take advantage
of opportunity given
to so few fighters,
so you made your decision.
After four hours of talking,
you decided to pray
on the plane and pack a parachute
you wore on the way.
Arriving in Rome
you put on a display
of a swift and strong style
that defined Cassius Clay:
lightning-quick feet
dancing in the ring
and flurries of fists
that swarmed like bee stings.
Stinging Russia and Poland

"I don't care who you are, boy; get out of here!"

on the road to victory,
you gained gold-medal glory
in the year 1960.
Admired and loved
by your Olympic peers,
you soon returned home
to parades of wild cheers
that greeted you
as you stepped off the plane
with hundreds of people
all chanting your name:
"Ca-shus,
Ca-shus,"
they roared across Louisville.
But the welcome was short
because away from sport
the country you fought for still
put people, like laundry,
in two separate piles,
and forced you, a black man, to deal
with hate-filled words
spit into your ear,
like, "I don't care who you are,

boy; get out of here!"
With anger and hate directed at you
they tried to sucker-punch
  your pretty brown face.
But anger and hate, thrown like weak jabs,
couldn't knock out
a prince of black race.
Sparking fire inside,
fanning flames of black pride,
fanning flames of courage
and heart you would ride
while blazing your path
as you turned pro,
you burned with a fire
that set you aglow.
Fighting opponents and hatred
with two glowing gloves,
you spoke your mind freely
while radiating love.
A black prince perched
on the precipice of fame,
young Cassius, the world
would soon chant your name.

Sparking FIRE INSIDE, fanning flames of BLACK PRIDE

ROUND FOUR
MIGHTY MOUTH

"I am the greatest!
I shook up the world!
I don't have a
     mark on my face!
I'm pretty!
I'm a bad man!
You must listen to me!
I can't be beat! . . .

Louisville Lip leaps to life
just a few short years
after your first pro fight.
Braggin'
and boastin'
and callin' the round,
signifyin'
how your opponent would go down.
One
by one
by one
they all fell;
each time you were victorious
at the DING-DING of each bell.
Each victory you crept
closer to Sonny
Liston, the champion,
for title and money;

Sonny Liston,
an ex-con armed-felon
cop-beater who
destroyed his opponents
and bulldozed his way to
the top of the ladder
in the heavyweight division.
Taking his title
was your ultimate mission
as you focused your energy,
confidence,
and vision.
From Chicago to Denver
long before the fight,
you arrived on Sonny's lawn
and taunted him one night,
saying, "Come out of that door
or I'm gonna break it down,"

I'm the prettiest thing
that ever lived!"
**— CASSIUS CLAY, in the ring upon winning
his first heavyweight title**

leaving a lasting impression
of you as a clown,
leaving a lasting impression
of you as a madman,
an impression you performed
as part of your plan.
From that night on,
all the way to weigh-in,
you taunted
and teased
to get under his skin,
SCREAMING
to any and all who would listen,
"DESTRUCTION IN EIGHT
OF THAT CHUMP, SONNY LISTON!"
White writers wrote words
and scribes scribbled script
of Liston silencing
your big mouth with one hit,
hoping "their" Negro
would put you in your place
by shutting you up
and uglying your face.
Your dressing room crackled
with E-lectricity
while you, Malcolm X,
and your younger brother, Rudy,
knelt facing east,
praying to Allah
to give you strength for your battle

in the belly of the beast,
praying for strength
against a mountain of a man
you called "a big angry bear,"
taunting words used
to motivate you
to fight
because you were scared.
But with Allah as your guide,
your spirit inside
glowed with a fire
as the big moment arrived. . . .

"If God's with me, can't nobody be against me!"
—Cassius Clay

February 25, 1964

Miami, Florida
"Lay-deeeees aaand gentlemen,
welcommmme to My-ami, Flor-ee-dahh,
for the heavyweight championship
of the world.
In this corner, tha challenja
from Louie-ville, Kenn-tuckyyyy,
wearing the white trunks with the red
trimmmmm,
weighing in at two hundred ten and
one-half pounds,
age twen-ty-two,
standing at six feet three inches . . .
the formerrrr Olim-pick
light heavyweight champ-e-onnnn . . .
Cash-yus Clay . . . Clayyyy."
"BOOOOOOOOOOO!"

"Aaand his opponent
from Denvahhh, Colla-radooooh,
weighing two hundred eight-teen pounds,
wearing the black trunkssss with
white trimmmm,
standing at six feet one inch,
age thir-ty-one,
the heavyweight champ-ee-onnnn
of the worrrrllld . . .
Charles . . . Sonny . . . Liston."
"YAAAAAYYYYY!"

"YAAAAYY

"BOOOOOOO

"Clay versus Liston
for the world heavyweight boxing title. . . .
Good luck, gentlemen."

diNg-diNg!

Clay comes out,
circling the ring;
Sonny steps
and steps
and steps
and ZING—
his left jab catches air
as Clay disappears,
circling,
ducking,
bobbing and weaving,
bouncing on toes
with speed so deceiving
that jabs from Liston
only destroy air
as young Clay dances at will,
around the ring
like a fleet-footed cat
eluding a dog, until
a rock-solid right
ripples Clay's flesh
from a brown-leathered fist
and vibrates his chest,
shaking

and quaking Clay's heart,

rattling and rippling ribs in their cage,

splitting muscle fibers apart,

but Clay is unflinching.

He steps in closer,

grabs Sonny,

then hooks him

by his right shoulder

and pushes him off

to set Sonny up

for a long left jab in the face,

then ducks

a left,

a right,

and a left-hooking fist,

swung from a meat rack

that mightily misses

Clay's head by a mile.

Using speed and style

young Cassius Clay

dance-dances away,

then lets fly a flurry of fists,

right-left right-left right-left combo,

shots to the head with crisp

snap and sting

from brown leather gloves

that drop pain on Liston

like bombs from above

as the first round ends

with the sound of

DING-DING

ending the assault

of Liston in the ring.

As the fight goes on,

Clay continues to bring

the pain to Liston

while boxing with spring

in bouncing feet

that stop-start-stop

to set up punches

that POP-POP-POP

to the face, to the chin,

to the chest, to the gut,

back to the face.

LEFT-RIGHT

opens a cut

under Liston's left eye,

then bloodies the nose

of Sonny the champ

as Clay dances on his toes.

But Sonny charges in

intent on devastation,

swinging a wrecking-ball right

that wobbles the foundation

of the challenger, Clay,

who bounce-bounces away

quickly on instinct,

then puts on a display

of dazzling speed

and imposes his will

diNg-diNg!

with a barrage of blows

to Liston until

at the start of round five . . .

"Hold on, folks. . . .

Something is wrong. . . .

Clay is seated in his corner too long. . . ."

Some sort of substance

caught you by surprise,

as Liston's gloves

brushed across your eyes,

voiding your vision

and singeing your sight,

motivating you

to stop the fight.

"I can't see!

Cut off the gloves!"

you shout to a figure

hovering above,

an old pro

named Angelo,

who brought cool

and eliminated fears

by rinsing your eyes

then swabbing your tears;

he calmed you down first

then shouted in your ear,

"This is the big one, Daddy—we're not
    quittin' now!

Just stay away from him and run!"

A decisive moment
that defined your character
as you stepped up and spun
back into battle,
blind in your eyes,
with visions of gaining
the world heavyweight prize.
Measuring Sonny
with your left arm out
from a safe distance
kept you in the bout
just long enough
for your eyes to clear,
just long enough
for you to hear
the sound of the bell
ending the round,
giving you confidence
to take Sonny down.

War waged on
until a crucial decision
at start of the seventh,
when Liston threw the towel in,
ending the fight,
making you heavyweight
champion that night,
a victory cheered by only a few,
because prior to the fight
there were white writers who
insulted,
degraded,
and dismissed you
as a clown,
a windbag,
and uppity nigger too.

Cassius Clay,
age twenty-two,
the new
heavyweight champion on full view,
you
silenced them all
from center stage,
gloves high, mouth open,
shouting with glorious rage,

"EAT YOUR WORDS!
EAT YOUR WORDS!
I AM THE KING!
I'M THE KING OF THE WORLD!"

ROUND
FIVE
BLACK STAR RISING

"How can I kill
somebody when
I pray five times
a day for peace?"
—MUHAMMAD ALI

1964

You were king of the hill,

still

no respect was given

after you snatched your crown,

cuz

word on the street

wuz

you wuz down

with Black Muslims in the Nation
    of Islam,

therefore down

with angry black radicals,

therefore down

with angry black radicals who
    carried guns,

therefore down

with angry black radicals who carried
    guns and defied authority,

therefore a radical

threat:

Heavyweight champion
down with Malcolm X?

Cassius Clay...reborn as

You shed your slave name of Cassius Clay,
giving birth to a new belief
in Islamic religion,
reflected in your name
when reborn
as Muhammad Ali,
a Muslim name meaning
"Worthy of praise,
high-exalted one."
You sacrificed your champion status
to practice the teachings of Islam,
sacrificing your soul
to the will of Allah,
your sacrifice supported
by five sturdy pillars:
Shahada,
which means declaration of faith,
Salat,
which means prayer five times a day,
Zakat,
which means charity to man,
Siyam,
which means fasting from dawn
   to sundown
to cleanse the soul during the month
   of Ramadan,

and *Hajj,*
which means a pilgrimage to Mecca,
   the holy land—
pillars introduced to you
by way of a man
you met on the street
who was called Captain Sam.
He introduced to you
the teachings and plan
of Elijah Muhammad
to help all blacks stand
up against racism
dealt by white hands.
In Miami
in a mosque,
the Muslim house of worship,
Brother John, the preacher,
spit fire from his lips,
about inherited slave names
with no sense of black ancestry,
leading to an erasure
of racial identity.
Finally,
someone spoke
to you directly,
saying progress would come

by any means necessary,
a message you embraced
with your soul faithfully
as you joined to serve
Elijah honorably.
Elijah the Messenger
fed the teachings of
   the Nation
to hungry black souls
filled with years of frustration,
souls stung by hate
since the days of the plantation,
souls beaten like animals
in savage humiliation.
Your soul became alive
with a swelling of black pride,
feeding fire you ignited
from self-love deep inside,
a fire you spread
to other black folk,
who looked up to you
even as some wrote
you off as a racist
filled with hatred,
respected and rejected
for your outspoken nature.

MUHAMMAD ALI

But in 1967
when called to serve your country,
at war
in Vietnam,
you said **NO** to the army,
refusing to fight
an unknown enemy
for a country that treated you
with anger and hostility.
For an unknown cause,
you refused to kill
and simply stood still
when your name was called
to step forward and serve;
you stood all alone
with great courage and nerve,
because faith in Allah
and faith in your
religion of Islam
kept you from war.

U.S. GOVERNMENT 1

An undying faith
soothed your soul with relief
as you said **NO** to war
for religious beliefs.
Your refusal to fight
in the war in Vietnam
made the U.S. government
use you as a pawn
and put you—the Greatest?—
into your place,
stripping you of your boxing license
in all fifty states;
they then snatched your title
and said you disgraced
the American name
using your boxing fame
to play the religion card
in a patriotic game
of war.
Your
sentence for saying **NO**:
locked up for five years
behind prison doors—
five years never served
because of your
request for an appeal,
which provided you with time
to try the case again,
but still you couldn't climb
back into the ring
to fight to make money,
because you spoke out
and defied your own country.
You gave up your title
but showed what you stood for
when Allah moved your spirit
to say **NO** to war:
undefeated in the ring
and outside a hero.
Score: U.S. government 1–
Muhammad Ali 0.

MUHAMMAD ALI 0

ROUND SIX
POLITICS OF PEACE

"Joe Frazier is too ugly to be champ. Joe Frazier is too dumb to be champ. The heavyweight champion should be smart and pretty like me." —MUHAMMAD ALI

Time ticked off on the clock
as your appeal awaited,
but for three years you stood firm
as your message vibrated
into a country conflicted
over the Vietnam War,
as the body count of young boys
continued to soar.
You now earned a living
by speaking your mind
on college campuses
to students defined
as long-haired hippies,
who flashed the peace sign,
igniting a fire
in youth to change times.
Protests and pickets
and the power of TV

splashed your face everywhere
for all the world to see.
From New York to Japan
to Africa and Thailand,
eyes across the globe
witnessed you take a stand
when you said no to war
for religious beliefs
and defied your government
by standing for peace.
But standing for peace
meant sitting out of your sport
as you continued to fight
your battle in court,
a battle you hoped
would soon come to an end,
while the world wondered . . .
"Will Ali fight again?"

ROUND
SEVEN
"WHO YOU CALLIN' TOM?"

"And when we told Ali his jaw was probably broken, he said, 'I don't want it stopped.' Godalmighty, was that guy tough. Sometimes people didn't realize it because of his soft, generous ways, but underneath all that beauty, there was an ugly Teamsters Union trucker at work."

—DR. FERDIE PACHECO, Ali's fight doctor after his jaw was broken
  by Ken Norton in the second round of their first fight

Politics and money
put you back in the spotlight
when promoters and politicians
arranged for you to fight
in Georgia,
a state without a commission
for boxing, while you
awaited a decision
from the government
allowing you
to refocus your vision
of moving up the ladder
to continue your mission
of reclaiming the crown

taken away from you.
Your path back to glory
now traveled through
Smokin' Joe Frazier,
the man who was the new
title-belt holder,
who stood undefeated
in the ring, but without fighting
you, he felt cheated,
a feeling shared
by you during your layoff,
feelings that generated
interest and a payoff
of the largest sum

of money for one fight:
two and a half million
dollars each for one night.
But before a big payday
and battle with Joe
for the heavyweight title,
you first had to show
the world you could still
fight like a king
and quiet the questions
regarding your sting.
Your first entrance back
into the ring in three years
sent waves of emotions

and an eruption of cheers
into a star-studded crowd,
who offered their loud
unwavering support
as you stood tall and proud
with all eyes focused
on you in the spotlight,
with all eyes focused
on you, the Black Knight,
as your eyes focused
on your opponent in the bout,
Jerry Quarry, who you
proceeded to knock out
in round number three,
working slowly but smartly,
showcasing your genius
for the world to see,
showing the world you could still
sting like a bee.
One more fight won
by one more knockout
set you up
for the title-crown bout
with fearsome foe
Smokin' Joe,
one child in a family of thirteen,
raised on a farm in South Carolina,
who found a profession in the ring
while working to learn
his trade as a meat cutter
in Philly at age seventeen.

Meat cutter became boxer
and boxing became a way
for a young high-school dropout
to someday score a payday,
a payday that arrived
versus you, Ali,
in a fight that was dubbed
"The Fight of the Century."
But prefight hype
turned sinister and ugly,
when you insulted Joe
with words that cut viciously
to the heart of a warrior
and proud black man,

calling him ignorant
and stupid
and a tool of the white man,
cutting even deeper
into his heart by dropping a bomb,
by insulting his blackness
when you called him Uncle Tom.
Uncle Tom!
Uncle Tom—
a degrading term
taken from a book
about a slave named Tom
who accepted and took
beating after beating

from his master, who was white,
but constantly forgave
and never put up a fight.
So, in describing Joe
you painted him in light
as a black "white hope"
who represented whites,
painting an ugly picture
with words to spotlight
Joe as a villain
in the ring despite
his raging black fury
he showcased in fights,
a fury fueled by fire

aimed at you for one night.
Two contrasting men
with contrasting styles
finally collided in the ring:
Joe the Patriot
versus you, the Draft Dodger,
his hook versus your bee sting,
Joe the Baptist
versus you, the Muslim.
Only one
would soon be crowned king.
The action began
as each of you planned
a way to attack

and knock out your man.
You bounced and circled
the ring in a dance
with Joe crouched in hiding
while trying to land
a bell-ringing hook
swung from his left hand,
but you shifted and shuffled
and battled his plan
with jabs of your own
thrown from lightning-quick hands.
Back and forth,
forth and back,
you each showed your skill,

seesawing the outcome
through fourteen until
the fifteenth and final
round saw you
battling
and battling
and battling through
the fury of a man
you insulted and degraded,
disrespected, teased,
and deeply humiliated.
Frazier was determined
to shut you up that night
by knocking you out

and ending the fight,
but the clock was ticking
as you entered fifteen.
Still Frazier continued
to search in the ring
for timing and space
to end the chase
of the Butterfly who insulted
his pride in black race.
Out of nowhere like lightning
came a leaping left hook
filled with Uncle Tom anger
as Frazier's fist shook
your brain in your skull,
snapping your neck back,
when his fist met your jaw
with one mighty

CrACK!

sending millions of ants
into your body as the mat
rose up to smack
your beaten brown back.
But as fast as the hook hit,
you bounced up again
with a swollen right jaw
and began to suck wind

YOU versus **George Foreman** for the championship fight

while waiting on the ropes,
as the ref counted three,
to re-enter battle
and deal with more fury
from Frazier, who continued
to pound away brutally,
at head,
at face,
at midsection and kidneys.
You jabbed
and dodged
and fought in the ring
through fifteen rounds
until the final DING-DING,
ultimately losing by unanimous decision
to Joe Frazier, still champion
of the heavyweight division,
a champion who earned
the coveted crown,
while you earned respect
when knocked to the ground
by getting back up
to finish the fight.
Your first loss in the ring
symbolized your life,
as you stood back up
with courage and pride
and became a symbol
for strength worldwide,
a strength that led
to a win outside sport

when you emerged victorious
in your battle with the court.
An overturned decision
kept you out of prison
and allowed you to focus
on your title-belt mission,
a mission
that began
in Texas and traveled
across distant lands,
like Switzerland,
Canada,
Ireland,
and Japan.
Ten fights,
ten wins,
all led up to Ken
Norton, a boxer
and former marine who
posed a big problem
for you in round two
when his rock-solid fist,
released from way back,
slingshot your cheek
and broke your jaw with a CRACK,
pooling your mouth with blood,
marinating your mouthpiece;
you continued to fight
using your ring expertise.
Guarding your jaw and spitting
blood through ten

rounds, you fought
until the bitter end,
fighting through pain
because this battle with Ken
was just one of many
you needed to win
for a shot
at the heavyweight title again.
But Norton still won,
changing your path to the crown
now held by George Foreman,
who six times knocked down
Smokin' Joe Frazier,
taking his title away,
providing *two* dragons
for you to slay,
a new one for the title,
an old one for revenge,
but the path back to your belt
had to begin
with a rematch with Norton,
which you went on to win.
Two fights later
saw you in the ring again
versus Smokin' Joe Frazier,
who you slayed by decision.
A twelve-round victory
returned you to the spotlight:
you versus George Foreman
for the championship fight.

diNg-
diNg!

ROUND EIGHT

THE BULL MEETS THE MATADOR

"You think the world was shocked when Nixon resigned?
Wait till I whup George Foreman's behind.

Float like a butterfly, sting like a bee,
His hands can't hit what his eyes can't see.
Now you see me, now you don't,
George thinks he will, but I know he won't.

I done wrassled with an alligator,
I done tussled with a whale,
Only last week I murdered a rock,
Injured a stone, hospitalized a brick,
I'm so mean I make medicine sick."

—MUHAMMAD ALI

Back to Africa
to reclaim your stolen crown,
in the country of Zaire
for the heavyweight showdown
of you versus George
Foreman, the champ, who
took the crown from Frazier
but never battled you.
Battling for a title
taken so long ago,
your fight versus Foreman
    got dubbed
"A Rumble in the Jungle."
Returning to roots
to take your belt back in the ring,
you returned to the roots
of warrior kings,
whose roots in return
burrowed into
your blood,
your soul,
and your spirit too
when African voices
shouted your name
with a native-tongue chant
as you stepped out of the plane:

"Al-ee, boo-ma-

"Al-ee, boo-ma-yay!
Al-ee, boo-ma-yay!"
words when translated
to English say,
"Ali, kill him!
Ali, kill him!"
making you the Hero,
making Foreman the Villain,
making you the People's Champ
because you were willing
to stand up to your country
and say NO! to war,
showing eyes worldwide
what a champ should stand for:
Pride,
strength,
and courage without fear
that showed your faith in Islam
was deep and sincere.
Your faith in Allah
glowed like a light,
burning within
stoking fire to fight
against ferocious Foreman,
a bull of a man,
who destroyed opponents

with bone-smashing hands
that hammered at flesh,
tearing muscles apart;
friends feared that Foreman
would tear *you* apart.
But the "Rumble in the Jungle"
missed its first fight date
when a cut to Foreman's eye
caused a thirty-five-day wait,
providing extra time
for you to prepare
and rally Africans
across the country of Zaire.
"Underdog Ali
is not the fighter he used to be.
He can't float like a butterfly.
He can't sting like a bee.
He can't move quite as fast,
can't dance anymore;
Foreman will flatten
his face to the floor,"
reported reporters
and scribbled scribes;
several picked
round one for your demise,
but only you knew

you had a surprise,
a Matador plan
that began
with quick feet that would dance
circles around the Bull
while setting up your hands
to stab
and jab
and stick-stick-stick
into Foreman's face
quick-quick-quick.
But Foreman practiced too
and listened to you
tell note-takers taking notes
what you would do.
So . . .
his plan
was to cut off the ring,
catch you
and corner you
on the ropes
then free-swing
at head,
at face,
at body,
and sides,

YAY!"

with determined destruction
that could hospitalize
you, a fighter-father-husband
and black man,
but no one knew you
had a surprise:
Foreman would be the Bull
and you the Matador
trying to tame an animal
to reclaim what was yours.

October 30, 1974

Kinshasa, Zaire

Africa

"Good evening, everyone, and welcome
to Zaire.
We are here to witness the battle for the
heavyweight championship of the world.
Each fighter will receive a handsome prize
of five millllllllllion dollars.
And nowwwww . . .
innnnnnnnnn this cornaaa . . .
weighing in at two hundred sixteeeeen
poundsss,
from Louie-villllle, Kenn-tuckyyy,

at thirty-two years of age,
with a record of forty-four winssss,
thirty-one by knockout, with two losses,
wearing the white trunkssss with the
black trimmmm . . .
Moe-hammadddd Al-eeeeeeee."
"Al-ee, boo-ma-yay!
Al-ee, boo-ma-yay!"
"Andddd . . . in thisss cornaaa . . .
weighing in at two hundred twenty pounds,
from Marshallllll, Teck-sisssss,

at twenty-five years of age,
with a record of forty wins, thirty-seven by
knockout, with no losses . . .
wearing the red trunkssss with the
white trimmmm . . .
Georrrrr-ge Foremannnn."
"BOOOOOOOOOOO!"

"Georrrrr-ge Foremannnn"

"BOOOOO

Gleaming golden prince
bounce-bounces feet in ring,
stops,
raises gloves,
bows head in prayer,
turns to Foreman . . .
DING-DING!

Muhammad the Matador
sweeps across the ring,
left to right,
right to left,
shifting,
and circling
Foreman the Bull,
who walks into a left-right
combo to the forehead,
like a red cape in flight.
Charging
and charging
and charging, the Bull comes
in on the Matador,
who takes the Bull by the horns.
The Matador lassos
the Bull in his grip,

tying him up
while shooting off his lip,
shouting,
"Come on, George.
I thought you could hit!"
The nose-snorting,
bone-smashing
Bull focuses force,
emerging from the grip
to throw the Matador on the ropes,
slashing hooks to the body
that tear into sides,
shooting shots into the Matador
that shake organs inside,
chattering teeth
and quivering heart,
taking tightly wound muscle fibers
and ripping them apart.
But the Matador bounces
side to side and up and down
on the ropes, absorbing blows
until DING-DING ends the round.

Breathe. Relax.
Relax. And breathe.
The nightmare that has haunted you
is now reality.
Yes, Foreman is strong,
yes, Foreman hits hard,
but nothing can hurt you
when strengthened by God.

"Come on, George. I thought you could HIT!"

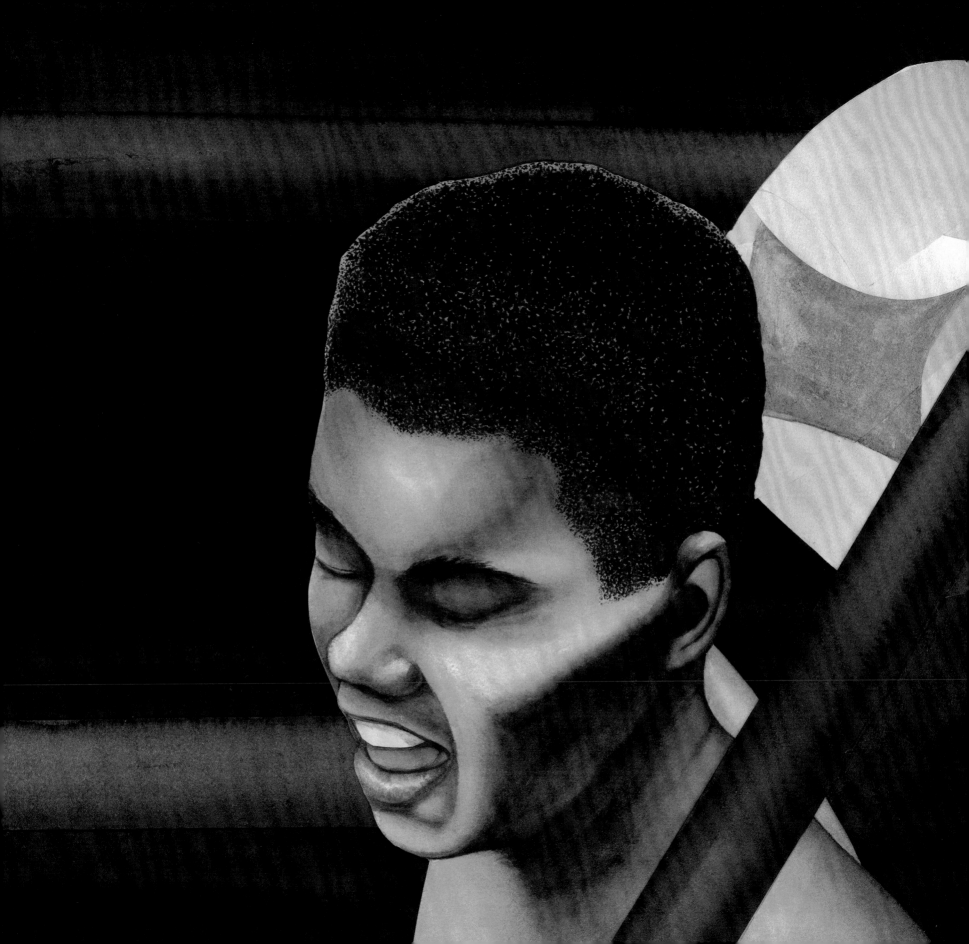

The time is now
to not think about you,
but what the power of winning
the title belt can do:
uplift black people living on welfare,
uplift black people with no
    knowledge of self,
uplift black people who can't afford
    to eat,
uplift black people sleeping on concrete,
uplifting all people
by taking your title into the streets,
but first you must focus,
FOCUS
and beat
the Big Bad Bull,
by becoming God's tool;
eyes focused, no fear
as you rise up from the stool,
turning to the crowd,
waving your fist in the air,
inciting African brothers
in the country of Zaire
to scream,
to shout,
to chant,
and say . . .

"Al-ee, boo-ma-yay! Al-ee, boo-ma-yay!"
"Ladies and gentlemen, this is quite
    a display—
just as Ali's chances in the fight
    look slim,
the people of Zaire
chant, 'Ali, kill him!'"
The second round
begins with a bad sign,
as the Bull charges in
and the Matador finds
the ropes brushing against his back
as the Bull goes on the attack
sending swift fist bricks
into his sides with a . . . THWACK!
But the Matador swaaaaaaaays
like a sail in the breeze,
grabbing the Bull by the horns,
pulling him closer to tease,
'IS THAT ALL YOU GOT?
IS THAT ALL YOU GOT?'
absorbing brick after brick,
taking shot after shot,
infuriating the Bull,
making his eyes see blood-red,
moving shots to the body
up top to the head.
Round after round
the Bull continues to pound,
free-swinging fists

hoping to knock down
a loudmouthed Matador
swinging in the ropes,
but the free-swinging Bull
becomes an outfoxed Dope
as the Matador's fists
become a red cape to steer
the Bull around the ring.
His power disappears,
from chasing and charging
and huffing and puffing;
the once-mighty Bull
is now a slow-motion shuffling,
wild-punching,
air-slicing
Bull hitting nothing.
Finally,
the Matador rises off the ropes
concluding the lesson
in the art of Rope-a-Dope;
with just thirty seconds
to go in round eight,
the Matador moves in
as the Bull awaits his fate. . . .

ThWACK!

"IS THAT ALL YOU GOT?"

Toro! Toro! Toro! Let's go!
You big ugly Bull . . .
now this is MY show!
I prayed to Allah
to give me hope,
and he answered my prayer
when I roped you . . . DOPE!
There's gonna be one man standing
at the end of this bout,
and that'll be ME
when I knock you out!
Chump! You thought I was tired?
You thought I couldn't fight?
Well, deal with this, sucka . . .
deal with this right!
Thrown over your shoulder . . .
what, you thought I was through?
Sucka, I'm faster,
smarter,
and prettier than you!
So deal with these fists
smacking your ugly face;
I'm taking you down
for the crown
to represent my black race.

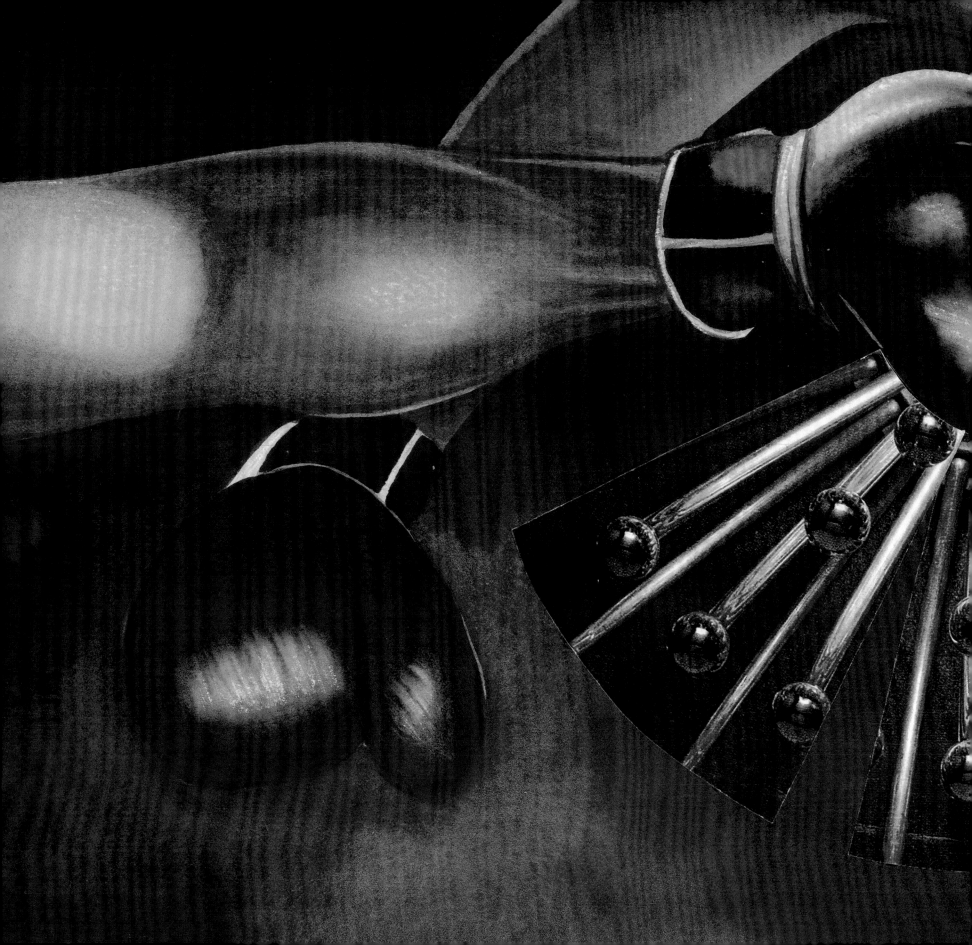

All I gotta do
is finish you,
so here's a right to the jaw
corkscrewing you to
the mat
on you're back.
You're done, sucka. . . .
YOU'RE THROUGH!
"Eighth-round knockout! Ali wins! Ali wins!"

A knockout, a knockout
by you in the eighth round
toppled Big Bad Bull
to reclaim your stolen crown,
completing a journey
that spanned seven years,
filled with love,
blood,
sweat,
and tears,
a journey completed
in a moment of sheer
inspiring glory
amidst warrior-king cheers.

"YOU'RE THROUGH!"

ROUND
NINE
GORILLA WARFARE

"I hated Ali. Twenty years I've been fighting Ali, and I still want to take him apart and send him back to Jesus."
—JOE FRAZIER

From Prince of Pugilism
to newly crowned King
of the World, your reign
extended beyond the ring;
from the slums of Chicago
to the shanties of Zaire,
your return to glory
lifted hearts everywhere.
Still you wanted,
needed,
savored another bout
with Joe Frazier to erase
any lingering doubt
about who was the real
champ between two
gladiators in the ring:
Smokin' Joe or you?

So you set the stage
for two titans who
tussled twice in New York,
but for the third fight you flew
off to the Philippines
for a battle between you
and your old nemesis Frazier,
a warrior you knew
would come prepared
to the ring, ready to die,
determined to dismantle
you and break the tie;
the first fight saw
his left hook knock you down,
not out, but hard enough
for Joe to keep the crown.
The second fight saw

you battle to the end
and outscore Frazier
on points to win.
But a fight
wasn't a fight
until you christened it in rhyme,
so "The Thrilla in Manila"
became a battle for you to shine.
The prefight hype
saw a repeat of the first,
but the hatred from Frazier
toward you became worse
as you constantly continued,
from the States to Manila,
to pound a black doll
you called "Frazier the Gorilla."
But Smokin' Joe channeled

his pain into fists,
anxious to unload
a leaping left hook to kiss
your pretty brown face
to the cold gritty mat
and tattoo canvas
on your cheek with a

SPLAT.

Focusing fire and fury
into his fists for one night,
Smokin' Joe was determined
to smoke *you* in that fight.

October 1, 1975

Araneta Coliseum

Quezon City, Republic of the Philippines

"Here comes Ali. . . . Here comes Ali!"

Draped in a white satin robe
trimmed in powder blue,
the majestic monarch
wades confidently through
an anxiously awaiting
fight-salivating crowd,
each step toward the ring
sending ripples of loud
thunderous applause
that rise into a roar,

as the monarch marches slowly
toward the ring to wage war.
Taunting and jawing
with each other in the ring,
each fighter pounces
at the sound of . . .
DING-DING!
Hands held high,
Ali creeps in close,
as Frazier crouches to avoid
Ali on his toes.
Measuring
and focusing
with fast hands and vision,
Ali detonates left jabs
to Frazier's head
with precision,
exploding red-leather bombs
with timing and skill,
but Frazier fights to get closer
by pushing on still,
slipping and sliding
and bobbing and hiding,
left to right,
right to left,
dodging leathered lightning.

diNg-diNg!

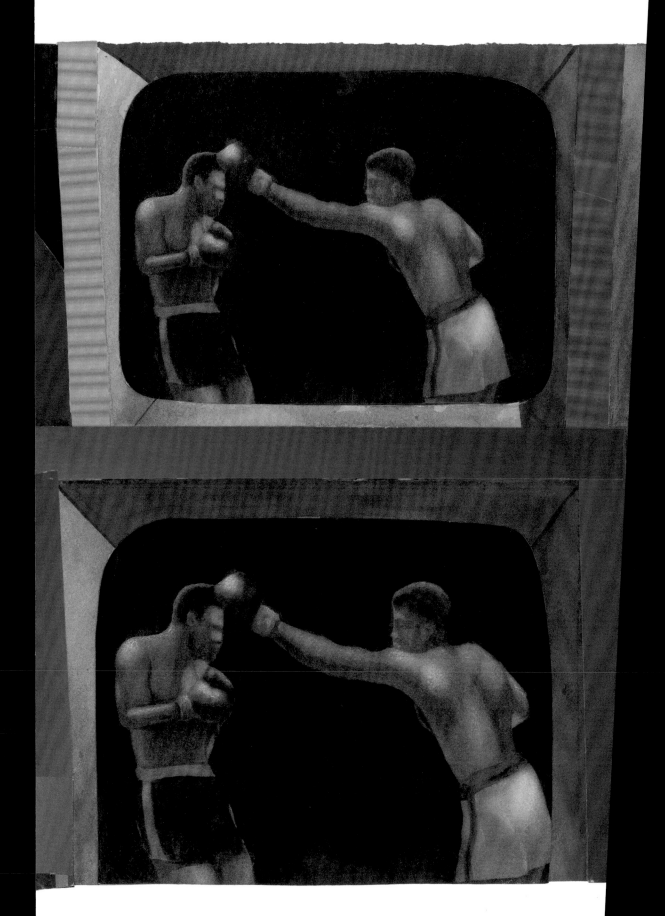

slipping and sliding and bobbing and hiding, left to right, right to left, dodging leathered lightning

But Frazier is unfazed
as Ali's head shots graze
his eyebrows,
his nose,
his jawbones and face,
forcing Frazier to focus
on Ali in a hurry.
With just twenty seconds left,
the champ lets fly a flurry
of fists aimed at Frazier,
determined to knock him down,
but Smokin' Joe smiles
as DING-DING ends the first round.
Round two is a repeat
of round one, but round three
sees Frazier slashing hooks
to the body of Ali,
smoking shots to the sides
of Ali as he hides
on the ropes,
gloves up,
taunting Frazier, who tries
to damage,
destroy,
pound,
and pulverize
the champ's organs inside
as the crowd stares
open-mouthed and mesmerized.
Through thirteen rounds
Ali seems to be winning

diNg-
diNg!

although each fighter endures
assorted bell-ringing
shots pushing pain
into brain
with skull-stinging
speed and power
thrown in the heat of battle
as rib cage,
kidneys,
and hot lungs rattle
from earth-quaking fists,
sending shockwaves to the heart,
as Ali and Frazier
tear each other apart.
Smokin' Joe sits
awaiting the start of round fourteen,
guzzling water,
spitting blood,
as his corner men clean
a cut under his right eye,
focused across the ring
at Ali, who sits
sucking air that stings,
waiting to wage war
at the sound of . . .
DING-DING!

You have ascended the mountaintop
and must now reach its peak;
your body is tired
but your spirit is not weak.

Your rubbery legs
carry you to meet Joe,
but your weighted-down fists
manage to strike blow
after blow
after blow
after blow
to your opponent . . .
Joe Frazier, who pushes
you to the summit.
Frazier pushes on
with lips swelled,
face cut,
blood in mouth,
vision blurred,
from eyes swollen shut.
Smokin' Joe fizzles out
with just one round to go,
his corner men ending
the fight when they throw
in the towel —
ending the fight,
remaking you
champ that night.
Raising your fists,
you then oozed to the floor,
as Frazier had pushed you
to the porch of death's door.

diNg-
diNg!

ROUND
TEN
GOING THE DISTANCE

"Every morning when I wake up as long as I live, whether the sun is shining or it's raining or snowing, I'll be three-time heavyweight champion of the world. That's worth taking some pain and hurt."

—MUHAMMAD ALI before his rematch with Leon Spinks

Coopman,
Shavers,
and Young,
Evangelista
and Dunn,
boxers you boxed with
in fights easily won.
But the fights were dull
and boring to see;
the world only wanted
to watch you, Ali,
come out and win
and put on a good show,
but your choice of challengers
was notches below
Liston,
Frazier,
Foreman,
and Ken
Norton, who you
battled again
for the third time through
a full fifteen to win.
You knew you weren't young,
but you still had the desire
to regale in the ring
and feed hungry fire,

so your search continued
for a slow easy foe
to provide a big payday
and maintain your glow,
a search that led you
to young Leon Spinks,
fresh easy money,
or so you would think.
His seven-fight pro career
brought little ink,
but an Olympic gold medal
put him on the brink
of stardom so
this fresh-faced pro
would step into the ring
to become your next foe.
But Leon was lightly
regarded by you,
as an untested young fighter,
inexperienced and new,
waging war in the ring
against you, the champ who
wrassled with alligators
and tussled with whales,
said no to your government,
to war, and prevailed.
To you Leon posed

no threat to possess
your belt, so you ate
more and trained less,
weighing in for the fight
at your heaviest yet;
the stage was set
for an unforgettable upset.
Age thirty-six,
you stepped back into the ring,
to fight a twenty-four-year-old
kid at DING-DING.
Lumbering slowly
over fifteen rounds,
you sat on the ropes, waiting
for Spinks to wear down,
but you outfoxed yourself
and never quite found
the energy needed
to defend your crown.
Battling and fighting
until the bitter end,
fighting off youth
no longer your friend,
fighting off Spinks,
hoping to win
the fight by knockout
or judges' decision.
But the knockout never came
before the final bell rang,
and the decision by the judges

ended your reign,
making young Leon
Spinks the new
heavyweight champ,
taking the title from you,
in an embarrassing loss
that saw Spinks earn
the belt, forcing you to shout,
"I shall return!"
Next night
after the fight
two A.M., under a streetlight,
you shadowboxed on the attack,
shouting,
"Gotta get my title back!
Gotta get my title back!"
You bounced and ran
at an exhausting pace
in the chilled air of February,
hoping to erase
your memory of the loss
and gain your ultimate place
as first three-time champ
to occupy space
in history books.
The whole world took
notice of your rematch
just seven months after,
hoping to observe
past glory recaptured.

Eyes worldwide witnessed
a repeat of the first bout,
as you won by decision
but left little doubt
that the time had come
to stop and get out
before Father Time
could score a knockout
of a fighter now slowed
but still filled with fire,
so nine months later,
you,
the Greatest,
retired.

**you,
the
Great
retired**

est,

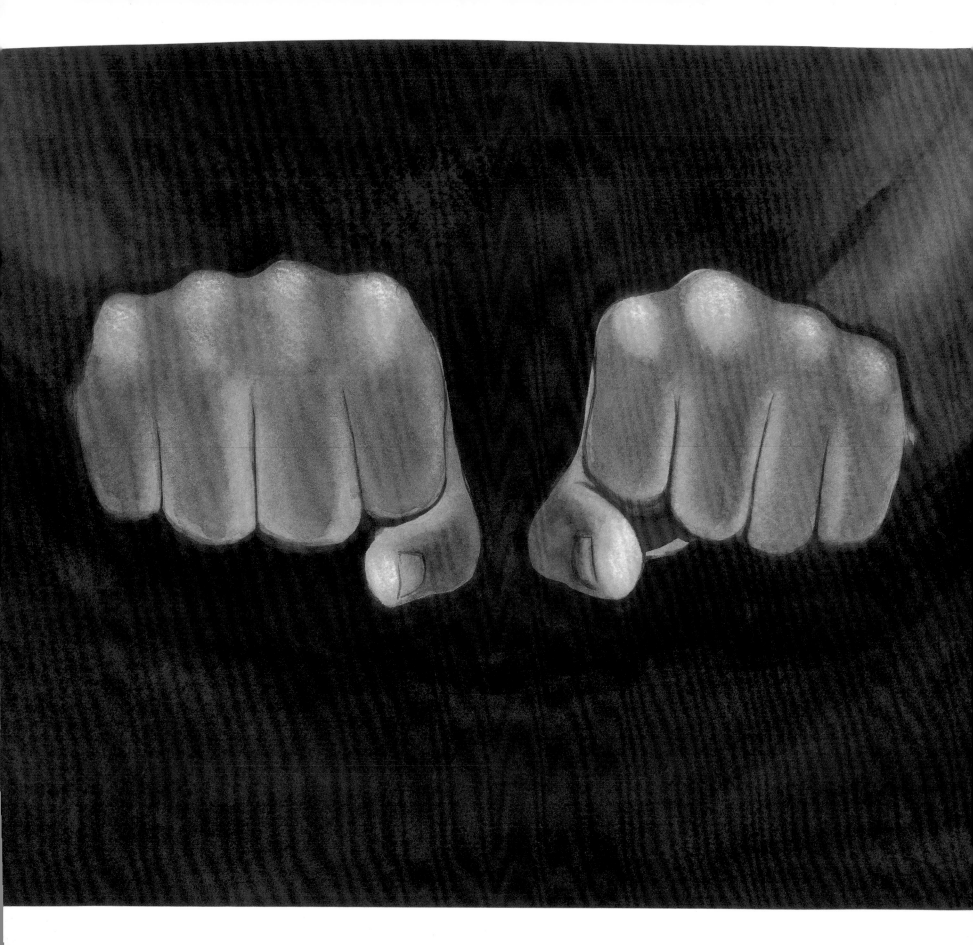

ROUND
ELEVEN
THE FLAME THAT FLICKERS

"He wanted to buy clothes for every person he saw in rags, pay the rent for every person on the street; feed every man, woman, and child who was hungry. And one man can't do it all. Governments can't do it; one man sure can't. But God knows Ali tried."
—LLOYD WELLS, longtime friend

First three-time champion
in division of heavyweight,
once tried by your own government
but now viewed as a great
boxer,
man,
tool of God, filled with love,
due to your mastery of skill
with two golden gloves;
two mighty gold gloves
that once rocked opponents,
controlled by a mind
that outthought opponents,

fueled by a mouth
that mocked opponents,
tools all used
to knock out opponents
with style,
strength,
smarts,
and speed.
Just twelve months retired,
you again felt the need
to shine under the spotlight
and take one last crack
at a fourth title belt

and make a comeback,
against wishes of friends,
against wishes of family,
urged on by your entourage,
who thought only of money.
One stood out
among your mixed motley crew,
an interesting, complex
character who
revived your spirit
in fights, between rounds,
a human bullhorn
named Drew "Bundini" Brown—

"Float like a butterfly,
sting like a bee"
some say was coined
by Bundini.
In the ring he motivated
you to be great,
but outside he caused
multiple headaches.
The lowest low came
when, down on his luck,
he pawned your title belt
for five hundred bucks
and took the money
to buy drugs and booze,
infuriating you
upon hearing the news,
so Bundini was banished
for five full years,
but you took him back
before your trip to Zaire.
You took him back
because you had love
in your heart,
unconditional,
taught from above.

Love in your heart
for your fellow man
allowed you to shine
in the spotlight and stand
up for what's right
and denounce what was wrong
in the world,
like poverty
and the war in Vietnam.
With three title belts
came a wealth of green,
never spent on yourself,
because wealth was seen
by you as a way
to help others out,
by you as a way
to feed hungry mouths,
by you as a way
to change others' lives,
but several stole from your wealth
in abundance from prize
money earned in the ring
over twenty long years,
making big-money paydays
quickly disappear.
So you stepped back in the ring
past your prime at thirty-eight
to replace dollars lost
and satisfy your great

hunger
and need
to shine in the spotlight,
hoping for glory
again to excite
hundreds,
thousands,
millions of eyes
focused on you,
watching a warrior's demise
in your last two fights
as your slow-shuffling feet
shuffled you slowly
two sad defeats.
Two sad defeats
in two fights
in two years,
brought a bittersweet end
to a glorious career,
brought a bittersweet end
that was too much to bear
as hypnotized eyes
dripped memory-soaked tears,
watching you wilt
without putting up a fight,
but your last losses in the ring
could not tarnish your light,
burning from a faith
on display throughout your life.

**burning
from a faith
on display throughout your life**

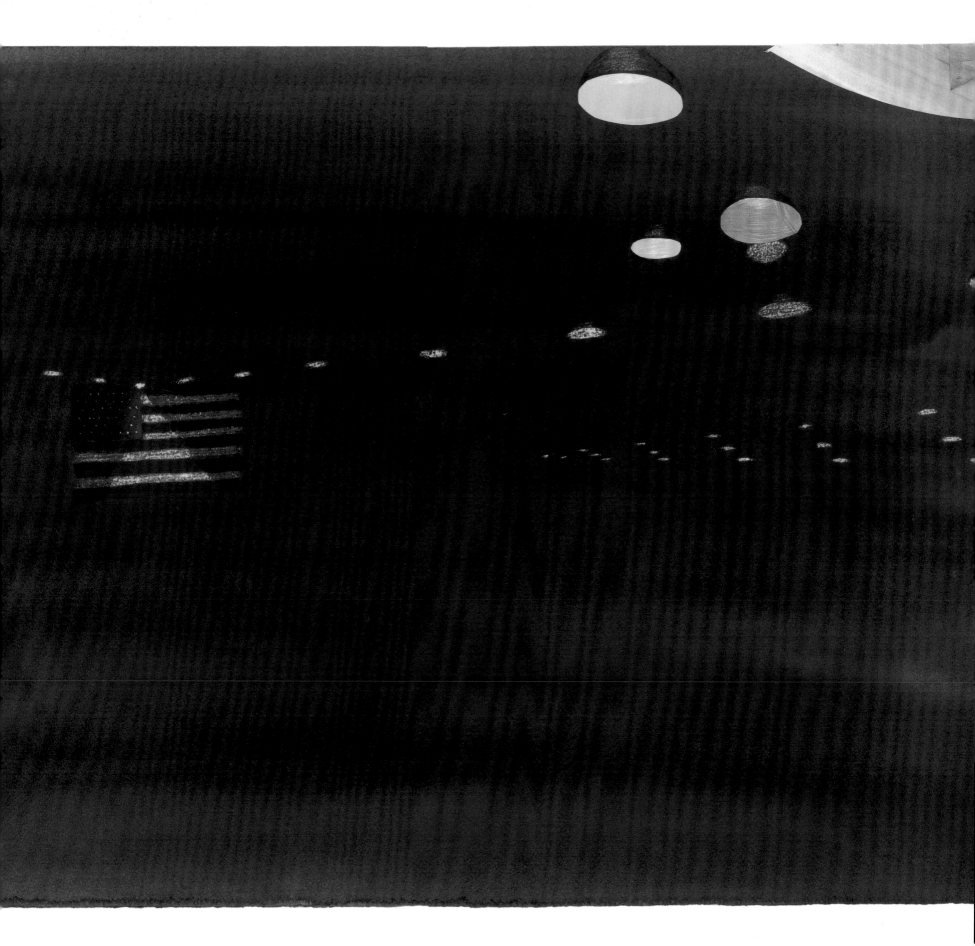

ROUND
TWELVE
MUHAMMAD
ON THE MOUNTAIN

"God gave me Parkinson's syndrome to show me I'm not 'The Greatest'—he is. To show me I have human frailties like everybody else does. That's all I am; a man."
—MUHAMMAD ALI, 1987

Outside of the ring
you were a husband and father
of eight lovely children,
one son,
seven daughters.
Your first wife, Sonji,
you met when you found
the light of Allah
and won your first title crown.
But the Islamic religion
is filled with tradition,
and strict rules for Sonji
filled your marriage with friction.

Belinda became wife number two,
a majestic Muslim who
shared the same faith as you,
bearing Maryum;
the twins,
Rasheeda and Jamilla;
and Muhammad Jr.
But then came Veronica—
last name Porche,
   like a car—
a beauty
who shined like a star,
splendidly sparkling
and shimmering in your eyes,
leading to the demise
of your marriage to
Belinda Ali,
soon making Veronica
wife number three.
She added two branches
to your family tree:
Hana and Laila,
like you, so pretty.
But years in the ring
began to wage war
inside your body
by slurring your
once-mighty words and
trembling your fists of victory;
the world began to wonder,

"What's wrong with Ali?"
and this struck a blow
to marriage number three.
Health questions and more
ultimately
brought a divorce to
Veronica and you,
now left alone
briefly in life,
no ring,
no glory,
no entourage,
nor wife.
You searched for someone
to share the love in your heart;
the search ended with Yolanda,
who brought a fresh start
to your life by turning
a long friendship into
a beautiful marriage
that fulfilled you.
Yolanda "Lonnie" Williams
was from Louisville too,
fourteen years younger
but a smart woman who
met you when she was
just a little girl,
when you became the
   heavyweight
champ of the world.

Your friendship with Lonnie
began long ago
and provided a strong base
for your relationship to grow,
closing a circle
of loves in your life,
as Lonnie saw you
evolve through each wife
and saw you mature
over time with three women,
two of whom bore
you six lovely children.
Later came two
more children who
were born out of wedlock
but were still loved by you.
Four wives,
eight children,
all given your love,
love strengthened by faith
in power above,
a faith that has you
five times a day
on knees,
head bowed,
to worship and pray
to the light of Allah
to guide you in life
with comfort and peace
through trouble and strife.

From Louisville Loudmouth
with a great gift of rhyme,
to a Beautiful Black Prince
who freely spoke his mind,
to a draft-dodging champ
who firmly declined
to take part in war
during segregated times,
you stepped up to challenge
authority with superior
strength, when blacks
were treated as inferior.
You stepped up to voice
what most could not say
because the light of Islam
guided your way
and strengthened your conviction
as you took a stand,
putting your faith
into Allah's hands.
But just what is faith?
How is it defined?
Is it love . . . ?
Is it trust . . .
in a spirit so divine?
Is it something you can touch?
Is it something you can feel?
Is it confidence in the truth?
Is it acceptance of God's will?

For each person faith
may be many things,
but faith in Allah
for you seemed to bring
peace,
love,
conviction,
and pride,
displayed throughout your life
and witnessed worldwide.
Known as the Greatest
for your great boxing skill,
your strength was now tested
by the strength of God's will
when the answer to the question:
"What's wrong with Ali?"
was diagnosed as
what turned out to be

Parkinson's syndrome,
a condition in you
that slows your walk,
slurs your speech,
and shakes your limbs too.
Your feet can still shuffle
and your mind is still sharp,
but the sight of you shaking
breaks many a heart.
Was it too many punches?
Too many blows
to the head,
to the body,
that made your motor skills slow?

"What's wrong with Ali?"

No one will know
for sure, but still
your life was a ride
that gave many a thrill,
through highs,
through lows,
up and down and nonstop,
all eyes were on you
when the thrill ride reached the top
of the magical mountain in 1996
on stage in Atlanta
to open the Olympics.
With vigorously vibrating limbs
you raised high
a flame that represented
your faith to the sky.
Holding the Olympic torch
with a warrior spirit,
you reignited memories
of the champ who never quit
in the ring,
in life,
using substance and style,
now a gentle gladiator
with a sparkling smile,
you lit the Olympic cauldron
glowing golden in the night
and became a supernova

bathed in beautiful light.

Time Line

1942

January 17 Born Cassius Marcellus Clay in Louisville, Kentucky

1954

October After his bike is stolen, young Cassius is introduced to boxing by local policeman Joe Martin.

December Wins first amateur bout

1956

Wins first title, a local Golden Gloves title

1958

Wins Louisville Golden Gloves

1959

Wins national light heavyweight Golden Gloves title

1960

Wins second Golden Gloves title

Wins gold medal at Rome Olympics

October 29 Wins first pro fight over Tunney Hunsaker in 6 rounds

December 27 Win by knockout (KO) over Herb Siler in 4

1961

January 17 Win by KO of Tony Sperti in 3

February 7 Win by KO of Jim Robinson in 1

February 21 Win by KO of Donnie Fleeman in 7

April 19 Win by KO of Lamar Clark in 2

June 26 Win by decision over Duke Sabedong in 10

July 22 Win by decision over Alonzo Johnson in 10

October 7 Win by KO of Alex Miteff in 6

November 29 Win by KO of Willie Besmanoff in 7

1962

February 10 Win by KO of Sonny Banks in 4

February 28 Win by KO of Don Warner in 4

April 23 Win by KO of George Logan in 6

May 19 Win by KO of Billy Daniels in 7

July 20 Win by KO of Alejandro Lavorante in 5

November 15 Win by KO of Archie Moore in 4

1963

January 24 Win by KO of Charlie Powell in 3

March 13 Win by decision over Doug Jones in 10

June 18 Win by KO of Henry Cooper in 5

1964

February 25 Wins heavyweight title by KO of Sonny Liston in 7

February 27 Announces that he is follower of Nation of Islam

March 6 Changes his name to Muhammad Ali, meaning "Greatly praised, high-exalted one"

May Takes a month-long trip to Africa

1965

May 25 Wins rematch with Sonny Liston by KO in 1

November 22 Win by KO of Floyd Patterson in 12

1966

February Requests deferment from military service

March 29 Win by decision over George Chuvalo in 15

May 21 Win by KO of Henry Cooper in 6

August 6 Win by KO of Brian London in 3

August 23 At a special draft hearing, Ali claims conscientious objector status based on religious beliefs.

September 10 Win by KO of Karl Mildenberger in 12

November 14 Win by KO of Cleveland Williams in 3

1967

February Ali's comment, "Man, I ain't got no quarrel with them Vietcong," is a major headline in newspapers across the United States.

February 6 Win by decision over Ernie Terrell in 15

March 22 Win by KO of Zora Folley in 7

April 28 Refuses induction into the Army

May 8 Indicted by federal grand jury; New York State Athletic Commission suspends Ali's boxing license; other states follow suit.

June 20 Ali is convicted by a federal grand jury of unlawfully resisting induction.

In order to support himself, Ali begins speaking at colleges across the U.S., which he continues to do for the next three years while on hiatus from boxing.

1968

May Ali's conviction upheld in court of appeals

1969

November Appears in Broadway show *Big Time Buck White*

1970

U.S. Supreme Court rules that conscientious-objector status is allowable on religious grounds alone; first step in Ali's return to the ring

October 26 Win by KO of Jerry Quarry in 3; first fight in 3 years

December 7 Win by KO of Oscar Bonavena in 15

1971

March 8 Loss, Ali's first ever, to Joe Frazier by decision in 15; Frazier retains heavyweight title

April 17 U.S. Supreme Court rules that all charges against Ali must be dropped.

June 28 Exactly fifty months to the day since Ali refused induction, the U.S. Supreme Court reverses his conviction.

July 26 Win by KO of Jimmy Ellis in 12

November 17 Win by decision over Buster Mathis in 12

December 26 Win by KO of Jurgen Blin in 7

1972

January Makes *hajj* (pilgrimage) to Mecca

April 1 Win by decision over Mac Foster in 15

May 1 Win by decision over George Chuvalo in 15

June 27 Win by KO of Jerry Quarry in 7

July 19 Win by KO of Alvin (Blue) Lewis in 11

September 20 Win by KO of Floyd Patterson in 8

November 21 Win by KO of Bob Foster in 8

1973

February 14 Win by decision over Joe Bugner in 12

March 31 Loss to Ken Norton by decision in 12

September 10 Wins rematch with Ken Norton by decision in 12

October 20 Win by decision over Rudi Lubbers in 12

1974

January 28 Win by decision over Joe Frazier in 12

October 30 Win by KO of George Foreman in 8 to regain heavyweight title—Kinshasa, Zaire

December 10 Visits White House at request of President Gerald Ford

1975

Converts from Nation of Islam to become a Conservative Sunni Muslim

March 24 Win by KO of Chuck Wepner in 15

May 16 Win by KO of Ron Lyle in 11

June 30 Win by decision over Joe Bugner in 15

October 1 Win by KO of Joe Frazier in 14 in Philippines

1976

February 20 Win by KO of Jean-Pierre Coopman in 5

April 30 Win by decision over Jimmy Young in 15

May 24 Win by KO of Richard Dunn in 5

June 25 Exhibition with professional wrestler Antonio Inoki
ends in draw after 15

September 28 Win by decision over Ken Norton in 15

1977

May 16 Win by decision over Alfredo Evangelista in 15

September 29 Win by decision over Earnie Shavers in 15

1978

February 15 Loss by decision to Leon Spinks in 15; loses heavyweight title

September 15 Wins by decision over Leon Spinks to regain heavyweight title

1979

June 27 Announces retirement from boxing

Travels to Africa to raise support for American boycott of
1980 Olympics in Moscow

1980

October 2 Loss to Larry Holmes by KO in 11

1981

December 11 Loss by decision to Trevor Berbick in 10

December 12 Retires from professional boxing

1984

Diagnosed with Parkinson's syndrome

1990

November Visits Iraq on a peace mission during Gulf War

1996

July 19 Lights Olympic flame in Atlanta, Georgia

1998

Named "Messenger of Peace" by the United Nations

2002

Visits Kabul, Afghanistan, on behalf of the United Nations

2005

November 9 Receives Presidential Medal of Freedom

November 19 Opening of Muhammad Ali Center, Louisville, Kentucky

December 15 Receives Otto Hahn Peace Medal, Germany

2007

June 5 Receives an honorary doctorate of humanities from
Princeton University

2009

December 3 Opening of Muhammad Ali Parkinson Center,
Phoenix, Arizona

CAREER RECORD
56 wins (37 by KO) **– 5 Losses** (1 by KO)
3 Heavyweight Titles